First published 2007
© Laurie Page, 2007

COUNTRYSIDE BOOKS
3 Catherine Road
Newbury, Berkshire

To view our complete range of books,
please visit us at
www.countrysidebooks.co.uk

ISBN 978 1 84674 017 6

Cover picture showing Clavering, near Saffron Walden
supplied by Bill Meadows

Photographs by the author
Maps by Gelder Design & Mapping

Designed by Peter Davies, Nautilus Design
Produced through MRM Associates Ltd, Reading
Printed by Borcombe SP Ltd., Romsey

Contents

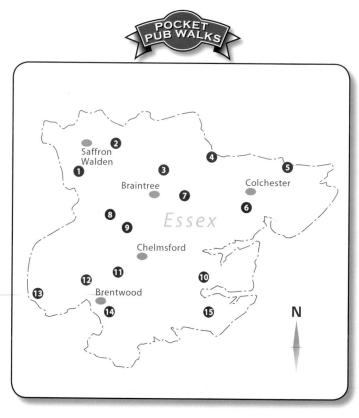

Area map showing location of the walks

Introduction

Essex has a wonderful variety of scenery, fascinating places of historical interest, ancient churches, thatched cottages and magnificent stately homes. All the walks in this book have something to enjoy along the way, as well as country paths and country air. Some throw new light on familiar places, such as the countryside that inspired John Constable. While others make excursions into tiny villages such as Stow Maries, Pleshey, Bures – or the inaptly named Ugley! And, while none have steep climbs up or down, Essex is not as flat as one might suppose, and the undulating landscape provides an opportunity to enjoy some wonderful views of tranquil rural and river scenes.

This is also a chance to relax and take advantage of the excellent hospitality offered by some of the best pubs in Essex. Some are renowned for their ales, others for the high quality of the food they serve. Most are old, traditional pubs, themselves historic buildings, and much loved by both casual walkers and keen ramblers alike. All these circular walks, of between 3 and 6 miles in length, begin and end at a pub and details of opening hours, food and drink are included. None of the walks is too arduous and even if you set off mid morning you should be back at the pub for lunch with time to spare! If using the pub car park while you do the walk, please consult the landlord first. There is also a note on places of interest nearby if you would like to make a day of it.

I would like to dedicate this book to my father who has been an enthusiastic walker all his life but who now suffers the ailments of age, preventing him from embarking on these adventures. He has encouraged me throughout and avidly spreads the news of my publications to friends and family!

I hope that you will gain as much pleasure and enjoyment from these walks as I did in devising them.

L. H. Page.

Publisher's Note

We hope that you obtain considerable enjoyment from this book; great care has been taken in its preparation. However, changes of landlord and actual closures are sadly not uncommon. Likewise, although at the time of publication all routes followed public rights of way or permitted paths, diversion orders can be made and permissions withdrawn.

We cannot, of course, be held responsible for such diversion orders and any inaccuracies in the text which result from these or any other changes to the routes nor any damage which might result from walkers trespassing on private property. We are anxious though that all details covering the walks and pubs are kept up to date and would therefore welcome information from readers which would be relevant to future editions.

The simple sketch maps that accompany the walks in this book are based on notes made by the author whilst checking out the routes on the ground. However, for the benefit of a proper map, we do recommend that you purchase the relevant Ordnance Survey sheet covering your walk. The Ordnance Survey maps are widely available, especially through booksellers and local newsagents.

1 **Ugley**

The Chequers

The **pleasant countryside** surrounding Ugley belies its name and there is plenty of interest on this walk. Look out for the wild deer in Broom Wood as you set off from Ugley, before passing Rickling Hall, now a farm but originally a medieval manor house. Then the route takes you on to the village of Quendon, with its pretty church, before returning to Ugley. There are many thatched buildings and attractive cottages to enjoy along the way.

Distance – 4¼ miles.

OS Explorer 195 Braintree and Saffron Walden. GR 513288.

There are a few stiles but the walking is generally easy.

Starting point The Chequers pub on Cambridge Road at Ugley.

How to get there Ugley is on the B1383 about 2 miles north of Stansted Mountfitchet heading towards Newport. Walkers must make arrangement with the landlord if they wish to use the pub car park. Otherwise, park further up Patmore End Road, the turning off the main road which runs alongside the Chequers.

THE PUB The **Chequers** is known as the 'Beautiful Ugley Chequers'! An inn since the 16th century, it is now a restaurant and a hotel as well as a pub. There is a separate restaurant serving a vast array of food including good home-made dishes of meat pies, lasagne and chilli, plus salads, a wide selection of fish options and a varied vegetarian menu. Not forgetting the specials board and roasts on Sunday! The ales include Speckled Hen and there are seven white and seven red wines on the menu to choose from.

Open 11 am to 11 pm every day. Food is served from 12 noon.
☎ *01799 540387*

1 Opposite the **Chequers**, on the other side of the road, go over the stile that takes you through **Broom Wood**. Follow the yellow

arrows. The path swings right then over a little wooden bridge and over a stile into a large field. Here go left, then immediately right along a wide grass path, keeping the hedge to your right. The route S-bends to a footpath T-junction. Turn right, going underneath the pylons to **Brixton Lane**.

2 Turn left up the lane and continue to where the pylons bridge the road. Here take the footpath on the right, lined on both sides by trees. This is part of the **Harcamlow Way National Trail**. Continue into a field and as the hedge ends, go left and proceed to the other side of the next hedge and through the opening on

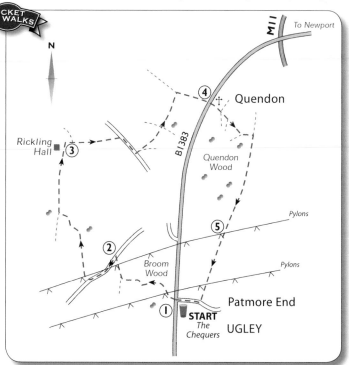

Essex

One of the pretty thatched cottages in Ugley.

the right. After a short while the buildings of **Rickling Hall** can be seen straight ahead. The path swings left to a footpath sign by the farm track. Go right down the track, heading towards the hall.

3 A concrete track takes you through the estate and into the surrounding buildings. **Rickling Hall** still has scant remains of a fortified building, but it is difficult for the walker to get a close up view of the house today. Take the path on the right between two large corrugated sheds. Keep to the right of the hedge. This path brings you to the road and a thatched cottage. Turn right. To avoid walking along the road you may wish to opt for the wide grass path by the field on the left. At the **Rickling Green** 'welcome' sign take the bridleway on the left. Keep to the main track for nearly ½ mile. As the path bends to the left, before passing over a ditch and going uphill, turn right (almost a U-

turn), going up a grass path which swings round the side of a cottage to the road at **Quendon**.

4 Turn right and then left up the path to pretty **Quendon church**. There is a choice of paths at the end. Take the one straight ahead which says 'Bridleway'. This swings right to a junction. Go left through a crop field and bear left again when you reach the trees. This takes you to a T-junction with a distant view of the motorway ahead of you. Turn right. Continue down this wide grass path for about ½ mile, keeping the trees of **Quendon Wood** on your right.

5 After you pass under the pylons and go through a hedge, veer right following along the edge of the field. After a short while, go over a stile on the right and into a meadow. Initially head towards the next row of pylons keeping a wire fence on your left, but about halfway down the field, walk diagonally across the middle towards the thatched cottages where there is a metal gate which opens (with some difficulty) onto the road. Turn right, bringing you back to the main road and the **Chequers** pub.

Places of interest nearby

Two miles south, in the town of **Stansted Mountfitchet**, is an excellent reconstruction of a Norman motte and bailey castle. Waxwork figures and exhibitions illustrate the story of domestic life during the 12th century. Animals such as goats, deer and chickens roam the grounds.
☎ *01279 813237*

Next door to the castle is the fascinating **Toy Museum**. It has a collection of toys and games from all ages and examples of many of these can be purchased in their Collectors' Shop. There are displays for film and theatre and also seaside pier amusements.
☎ *01279 813567*

2 Hempstead

The Bluebell Inn

The quiet and attractive village of Hempstead makes an excellent base for this walk which offers views over the surrounding countryside and a wealth of Essex farms, including one moated farmhouse. The splendid pub and the church are interesting old buildings, both with links to the past. A hero of medicine, Dr William Harvey, is buried in St Andrew's, and the highwayman Dick Turpin was baptised there. There is a shorter option, but the full walk will take you to the pretty neighbouring village of Great Sampford and back again using parts of the Turpin Trail and some quiet little lanes.

THE PUB The **Bluebell Inn**, it appears, has been a pub for more than 400 years, although it has changed its name many times over the centuries. It is renowned for being the birthplace of the notorious highwayman Dick Turpin, whose father was the

Distance – 3¼ or 5 miles.

OS Explorer 195 Braintree and Saffron Walden. GR 634380.

Good tracks, but if there has been recent rain be prepared for some muddy paths in the later stages of the walk.

Starting point The Bluebell Inn, Hempstead, on the main road (B1054) that runs through the village.

How to get there *Hempstead lies on the B1054 between Radwinter and Steeple Bumpstead, about 6 miles east of Saffron Walden. Walkers may park in the pub car park with permission or park near the church.*

innkeeper in 1705 when Dick was born. Today, it is a freehouse of character. The regular ales on tap are Adnams Bitter and Broadside and Woodforde's Wherry, and there are usually two guest draught ales. There is a large selection of food, with a wide choice of club sandwiches but also some quality home-cooked pub meals such as beef and ale pie, Sunday roasts and a good selection of vegetarian meals.

Food is served from 12 noon to 3 pm and 6 pm to 9.30 pm Monday to Friday, and all day from 12 noon to 9 pm Saturday and Sunday. In winter the pub is closed all day Monday and closes at 7 pm on Sunday.
☎ *01799 599199*

1 Take **Church Lane** opposite the **Bluebell Inn**, which goes uphill to **St Andrew's church,** and turn left into the churchyard. Several eminent members of the Harvey family are buried in the

Essex

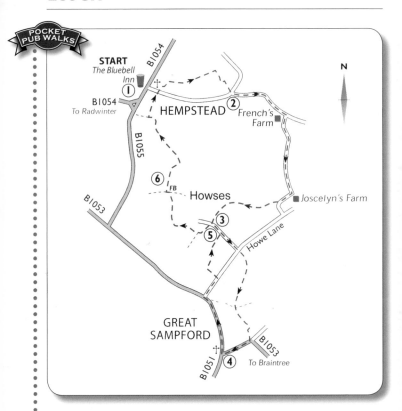

church, including Dr William Harvey who in the 17th century discovered the circulation of blood, and Admiral Eliab Harvey who captained the *Fighting Temeraire* at the Battle of Trafalgar in 1805. One hundred years before that, Dick Turpin was baptised here. The church is usually open to visitors. Bear to the right of the church building and through the trees on the right-hand side of the grounds is a path that leads to a stile (**Turpin's Trail**) and then goes across a field to a second stile. Go straight across this next field to the grass verge that follows the line of the hedgerow. At the bottom of the slope is a footpath junction. Turn right

Hempstead Walk 2

alongside the ditch. At the end, by the post, go left, crossing the ditch by the footbridge. The path swings right to the road.

2 Take the left turn, which goes uphill (not to Boytons) and passes **Pollards Cross Cottage** to your left. Proceed up this quiet lane to **French's Farm**. Stay right at the little road junction and continue for another ½ mile along the lane, passing **Joscelyn's Farm**. Soon after, by **Rose Lea Cottage**, where the road bends sharply to the left, turn right down the public byway. This is a wide dirt track where you have a view of **Hempstead church** in the distance. At the fork before the farm building, bear left to the road.

For the shorter walk, cross over and take the footpath opposite, following the instructions from point 5 below.

3 *To continue the full walk*, turn left down the road to the next junction. Go straight over along a wide footpath. There are good views of the surrounding countryside to enjoy here. The path swings right following the line of telegraph poles. At the junction at the end, go straight over, going gently downhill with the hedgerow to your left. At the bottom turn right towards the village of **Great Sampford**. When you reach the lane turn left and then right at the main road. You will pass the old school and **Red Lion** pub and come to a T-junction with the parish church in front of you.

4 Turn right up the main road and then along the walkway on the right that is raised above the road. Shortly after passing some pretty thatched cottages, turn right into **Howe Lane**, going gently uphill. Take the next footpath on the left, going up steps and into an open field. The path swings right, going around the edge of the field,

St Andrew's church, Hempstead.

and a little way up cross over a ditch through the opening in the hedge on your left and proceed on up to the cottages by the road. Turn left at this road towards the crest of the hill and the byway junction which you passed earlier in the walk (end of point 2).

5 Turn left along the public bridleway and follow the perimeter of the field. Look out for a stile in the hedge to your right, which leads into a horse field. There is a pond to the right. At the next stile by a moated farmhouse (called **Howses**) go left down the track leading from the farm. Cross a cattle grid and take the footpath on the right on the <u>other</u> side of the ditch. There are some good views to the left and **Hempstead church** can be seen straight ahead. Continue down the slope alongside the ditch until the path turns sharply to the left. Here, at the footpath post, cross over the stream via the footbridge.

6 Go up the steps to the field and turn left. Then almost immediately turn right before the next ditch, up an unmarked footpath which follows the edge of the field, swinging right at the end and then very soon, turning left through the hedgerow by the sign of the **Turpin Trail**. Cross the field heading towards **St Andrew's church**. Join another hedgerow at the corner and bear right over a stile. As the hedge turns 90° to the right, you go left through the hedge and across the corner of the next field to a stile at the wire fence. After crossing this bear slightly to the right to an old iron gate. Reach the road opposite the entrance to the church via another stile and at the road (**Church Lane**) turn left down the hill back to the **Bluebell Inn**.

Places of interest nearby

There is plenty to see at **Saffron Walden**, 6 miles to the west, including the magnificent Audley End House, now in the care of English Heritage.
☎ *01799 522399*

3 **Gosfield**

The Green Man

There is a little of everything on this walk. It begins from the village of Gosfield, and passes its ancient church before taking a footpath with a view of Gosfield Hall, a grand stately home that was a sanctuary for French royalty following the French Revolution. A walk through a disused airfield, built for the bombers of the American Air Force during the Second World War, and into woodland leads on into open countryside and to a nature reserve, before returning to the village pub, where some excellent food is on offer.

The **Green Man**, which has been a pub since 1839, is renowned for its food and for very good reason. The menu has an excellent choice, with food of high quality, such as their duck breast with plum and apple sauce. As well as the main menu, there are tasty snacks and specials on offer. The beers are Greene King IPA and Abbot, which can be consumed in a pleasant beer garden in the summer. There is also a good selection of wines.

Open 11 am to 3 pm (from 12 noon on a Sunday) and 6 pm to 9 pm. Food is served from 12 noon to 2.30 pm and 7 pm to 9 pm.
☎ *01787 472746*

Distance – 4¼ miles.

OS Explorer 195 Braintree and Saffron Walden. GR 784295.

Fairly flat, easy walking, with concentration needed when navigating through Broakes Wood.

Starting point The Green Man in Gosfield.

How to get there *Gosfield lies on the A1017 between Braintree and Sible Hedingham. The Green Man is on the main road on the southern approach to the village. There is parking available in the lay-bys in The Limes, the road opposite the pub.*

1 From the **Green Man** car park, turn right and walk up the main road for a little way to the **King's Head** pub at the next junction. Turn left up **Church Street** towards the lake and **Beazley End** and continue past the sports ground until you reach the little

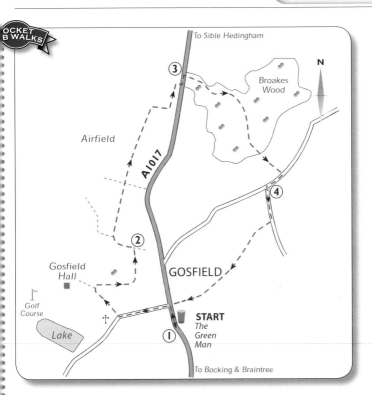

parish church of St Catherine, the present building dating from 1435. Here, in front of the church, take the narrow but well worn footpath on the right which cuts across the field. You will be able to see **Gosfield Hall** through the trees slightly to the left. No longer open to the public except by private arrangement, Gosfield Hall was first built in Tudor times but later became home to the French royal family after the French Revolution at the end of the 18th century. When you reach the end, turn right up the lane and look out for a footpath a few hundred yards down on the left, which goes through trees, alongside a fence. This path turns 90° right, then left and comes out into an open field.

Essex

Bocking windmill.

2 Turn left and continue along a grass path. At the next fork soon afterwards, bear right and at the end of the field turn left. This will bring you out onto a concrete track. Turn right and walk up the track. You are on part of the disused airfield, built in 1942 for US Bomber Command but closed just four years later after the end of the Second World War. Sadly there are no buildings left standing but a network of runways still exists and the walker follows the line of one such runway (the concrete track) for some distance. When you reach the parked trailers, bypass them on the grass path on the left. Continue straight over at the road and when you reach a metal gate, although there is no sign, you will see a grass path on the right going through the meadow and heading towards the main road. Take this path, which swings to the left at the end of the field alongside a wooden fence and runs parallel with the main road.

3 Where it eventually joins the main road, turn left keeping on the grass verge and after a short distance and before the 'welcome' sign for **Sible Hedingham**, cross the road and take a path on the right which is the entrance to **Broakes Wood**. Follow it to the car park and take the path by the map board which goes straight ahead. Follow this winding path through the trees, sticking to the main trail. At the next path junction go right into a more thickly

wooded area, following the red trail marked by the painted posts. At the next fork go right then immediately left, soon passing a pond. Turn right, then left and then go straight ahead ignoring any more turns. A field and a bank are to your left. This path terminates at the road. Turn right and continue past a school to the next road junction where you turn left down the lane.

Go gently uphill past the building called **Shardling** and immediately after this, on the right, take the stony footpath. This continues as a grass path with a field to the left and a hedge to the right. At the end of this field, carry straight on across the next. The narrow path takes you down to a stile by a brook which you cross and go up through a little wooded area. Bear left at the top of the slope and through a wooden gateway into **Gosfield Nature Reserve**. Take the path immediately on your right through the trees. As you come to the little footpath crossroads just before the lake, turn right, proceeding round two metal gates in succession and continue to the main road opposite the **King's Head** pub. Turn left down the road, back to the **Green Man** where you started.

Places of interest nearby

A few miles south of Gosfield, just outside Braintree is **Bocking Windmill**, a post mill dating from 1721. It is owned by the district council but opens up on Sundays during the summer.
☎ *01376 552525*

Just across the field from the windmill is **Doreward's Hall Open Farm**. There are sheep, goats, chickens and donkeys which you can feed by purchasing food from the well stocked farm shop, which also provides home-made produce such as cakes and jam, plants, vegetables and much more. There is a smuggler's maze to get lost in!
☎ *01376 324646*

The Eight Bells

This pretty village is divided by the county boundary, with Bures hamlet in Essex, where our walk begins, and Bures St Mary in Suffolk, the two separated by the River Stour. The route takes you over the Stour into Suffolk, and back into Essex past a 17th-century mill, before heading out into the countryside on a circular tour around the tiny community of Mount Bures, whose church tower stands as a landmark during the walk.

The Eight Bells is a 15th-century, timber-framed building which is now Grade I listed. It is a freehouse and there is an extensive menu of all the usual snacks, sandwiches and salads, plus a good selection of fish dishes, including trout and smoked mackerel. It has a specials board offering typical English dishes such as shepherd's pie and steak and ale pie. Tasty desserts include cherry and almond pie. All the food is very reasonably priced. The beer is Greene King Mild, Abbot and IPA, also Young's Bitter, along with Dry Blackthorn cider.

Open Monday to Friday 11 am to 3 pm and 5 pm to 11 pm, Saturday all day from 11.30 am to 11 pm and Sunday 12 noon to 10.30 pm. Food can be ordered between 12 noon and 2 pm and from 7 pm to 9 pm every day.
☎ *01787 227354*

1 From the **Eight Bells** continue along the main **Colchester road** (B1508) towards **Sudbury**. The road turns sharp right and over the **River Stour Bridge** into **Bures St Mary** in Suffolk. Turn

Distance – 5 miles.

OS Explorer 196 Sudbury, Hadleigh and Dedham Vale. GR 904339.

There are a number of stiles to negotiate.

Starting point The Eight Bells public house.

How to get there *Bures and the Eight Bells lie on the B1508 between West Bergholt and Sudbury. There is parking in the road, or if you are going to use the pub, with permission you can park in front of the Eight Bells.*

right after the church, towards **Stoke** and **Nayland**, and follow the road round to **Church Square**, with its ancient houses and cottages. Pass the football ground and just after the village hall, take a footpath on the right that goes across the field. At the other side of the field a gate leads out to the public footpath on the private road for **Bures Mill**, a 17th-century watermill once used for flour milling. Proceed down this road and at the fork bear right, which takes you close to the mill, round a fishing lake and over a stile into an open meadow.

2 Bear left and head towards another stile in the middle of a wire fence. Follow the path into a large field, over two more stiles and

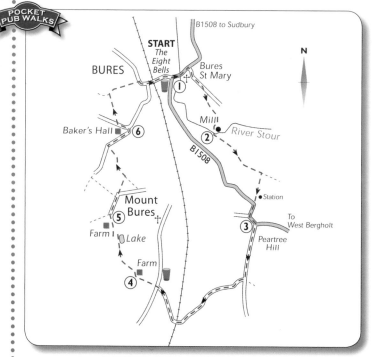

The 17th-century watermill in Bures.

a ditch. Just before the second ditch go right and a little way up on the left you will see a wooden footbridge, which you cross. Immediately turn right along a wide track passing the water sub-station and on to the road. Turn left (watch out for traffic) and after the next bend, go right down **Peartree Hill**.

3 Follow this for some distance past **Elms Farm** and when you reach the next little road junction go right, signposted to **Wakes Colne** and **Chappel**. After passing the thatched cottage of **Josselyns** you will get a view of **Mount Bures church** to the right. Follow the lane round over the railway bridge towards **Bures**. Continue on past **Takelys** to the main road. Here go straight over (**Fenn Barn**) along the track, towards the farm.

4 Go round to the left of the farm building and over a stile into a horse field. Walk down to the far corner of the field, through a metal gate and on down to a narrow gap in the fence by the lake. Turn left and a little way down go right over a footbridge and stile, following the footpath arrows towards farm buildings at the top of the slope. Step up over a high stile and cross a little field to the farm track by a large shed.

5 Turn right up the concrete track. You will get another view of the pretty church of **Mount Bures**. Continue up to where the lane veers sharply to the right, with a wooden gate and a stile in front of you. Go over this stile and follow the arrows over two more stiles, turning left at the bottom past the rusty coloured cottages. Proceed up to a little lane. Turn right up the lane to the road by **Baker's Hall**.

6 Turn left and after about 100 yards, opposite the farm sheds, go right along a footpath, through a thicket and over a bridge. Turn right and follow the path back to **Bures**. Turn right again when you reach the road and go under a railway bridge to the T-junction. The **Eight Bells** pub is just round the corner on the right.

Places of interest nearby

Four miles south of Bures are the **East Anglian Railway Museum** and **Chappel Viaduct**. The museum has a collection of steam locomotives and rolling stock on display as well as much in the way of railway memorabilia. The station buildings are essentially presented as they would have looked when they were built in Victorian times. The impressive viaduct, spanning the Colne Valley, stands in Chappel village nearby.
☎ *01206 242524*

5 **Dedham**

The Sun Inn

Dedham is a very popular, traditional Essex village, with the added attractions of an art museum, the Shakespeare Gallery, a magnificent parish church, a rare breeds animal farm and, of course, boating and canoeing on the River Stour. Not to mention Flatford Mill, a mile away, one of the locations made famous by John Constable, the landscape artist, who was born here. The walk begins along the banks of the Stour at Dedham Lock and explores the beautiful countryside that inspired not only Constable but also many other artists both past and present, returning along the valley of the Black Brook to the village.

Distance – 3¼ miles.

OS Explorer 196 Sudbury, Hadleigh and Dedham Vale. GR 057332.

Some gentle slopes in excellent walking country.

Starting point The Sun Inn, Dedham.

How to get there Dedham lies on the B1029 between Ardleigh and Stratford St Mary on the A12. The B1029 runs right through the centre of the village where the Sun Inn can be found. There is a car park through the arch and around the back of the pub which you can use with permission, or alternately, allocated parking spaces along the main village street.

THE PUB With four open fires and old oak beams, the **Sun** is an old coaching inn of character dating from the 15th century. It is now a hotel and freehouse, with an interesting menu. Customers can choose wood pigeon risotto, grouse, or select from a good fish menu including trout, halibut and scallops. The fruit and vegetables are produced by local growers and herbs come from the garden. The bar board has lighter snacks. There are four real ales on tap, Adnams Broadside, the award winning Brewer's Gold, plus two guest ales. The pub stocks no fewer than 40 wines.

Open all day 12 noon to 11 pm Monday to Saturday and 12 noon to 6 pm on Sunday. Food can be ordered from 12 noon to 2.30 pm (3 pm Saturday and Sunday) and 6.30 pm to 9.30 pm (10 pm Friday and Saturday).
☎ *01206 323351*

Dedham Walk 5

1 Turn left out of the **Sun Inn** car park and proceed along the village street, turning left up **Mill Lane**, so called because here once stood the mill owned by Golding Constable, father of the famous painter John Constable. Before the road bridge, turn left along a footpath which takes you over the river and **Dedham Lock**. After passing through the metal swing gate, go left along the grass path through the meadow (part of **St Edmund Way**). Bear right at the fork. The route soon follows closely the line of the **River Stour** on the Suffolk side. This pleasant stroll continues along the riverbank for about ½ mile via a wooden footbridge and eventually ends up at the main road.

2 Go through the metal swing gate and the tunnel under the A12. At a gate by the road, turn left past the 16th-century **Talbooth**

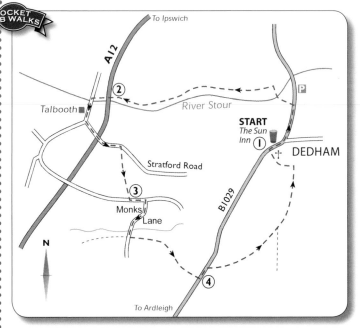

Dedham's parish church.

Restaurant and up to the road junction. Turn left along **Stratford Road**, passing back over the busy A12. At the bottom of the slope, opposite **Dalethorpes**, take the footpath on the right going over a stile. Go to the right of the wire fence, past massive oak trees and up over two successive stiles to the road.

3 Turn left and a little further down the road turn right into **Monks Lane** (No Through Road). As the road ends, continue down the public byway. By a ditch at the bottom, turn left onto an unmarked footpath into a field, following alongside the brook

on your left. Continue through a metal gate and at the concrete bridge bear right through another metal gate, still keeping the brook to your left and pass a tennis court and farm buildings to the road.

Turn left along the road and a little way up take the footpath on the right by a green metal barrier. The path immediately turns sharp left into a field and soon follows the line of the ditch. Follow the yellow footpath arrows. The tower of **Dedham church** can be seen to the left. After about ½ mile, another path joins from the right. Go straight on over the wooden footbridge and through three successive fields. You are now on the route of the **Essex Way**, marked by the sign of the red poppies. When you reach the cricket field go left to a children's roundabout and there go right down the tree-lined alley. This takes you to **Dedham** village street. Turn right to the **Sun Inn**.

Places of interest nearby

Dedham is definitely a place for lovers of art. Apart from the obvious connection with John Constable, just ¾ mile south of the village is **Sir Alfred Munnings Art Museum and Castle House**. A fine display of paintings by this early 20th-century artist and President of the Royal Academy is kept in fine surroundings at Castle House, which dates from the Tudor period although much of the present building is Georgian.
☎ *01206 322127*

The **Shakespeare Gallery**, in a 15th-century timbered building in Dedham High Street, features changing exhibitions of good local artists.
☎ *01206 322522*

6 **Layer-de-la-Haye**

The Donkey & Buskins

This is one of the longer walks featured in this book, taking advantage of some wonderful Essex scenery around the Abberton reservoir throughout the first half of the route. The reservoir is home for a variety of birds and wildlife. The route from Malting Green goes south to the pretty isolated parish church of Layer-de-la-Haye and towards Birch Green before returning to the village.

THE PUB The **Donkey & Buskins** is a privately-owned freehouse. The building dates from 1840 and has been a pub since 1911. There is a varied menu written up on boards around the walls. The fish selection includes sea bass and there are also good home-made traditional dishes. Some customers have a problem with the very generous portions for which the pub is renowned! The beer is Greene King IPA, along with changing

Distance – 5¾ miles.

OS Explorer 184 Colchester. GR 975208.

The walk follows mostly well trodden footpaths and tracks with more extensive road walking along country lanes towards the end.

Starting point The Donkey & Buskins pub at Layer-de-la-Haye.

How to get there *The Donkey & Buskins lies on the main road, the B1026, about 3 miles south-east of Colchester town centre just before the village of Layer-de-la-Haye. Walkers may use the pub car park with permission.*

guest ales, and a full range of wines. There is a pleasant beer garden to enjoy in the summer.

Open 11.30 am to 11 pm every day except Sunday when it opens at midday. Food is served from 12 noon to 2.30 pm Monday to Friday; to 9.30 pm on Saturday; and to 7.30 pm on Sunday.
☎ *01206 734774*

1 Take **The Folley** lane opposite the **Donkey & Buskins**, signposted to **Abberton**. A little way up on the left take the footpath down a tarmac track to the '**Black Barn**'. When you reach the **High Tec building**, follow the footpath sign along by the wooden fence. Go over an unusual metal stile and the path swings left past a little pond, taking you through the woods. Go over a wooden stile and through a metal gate. At the shingle path turn right going uphill. The stony path converts to a road.

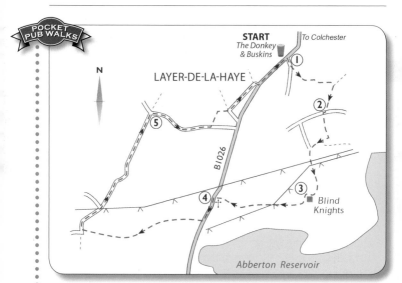

START | To Colchester
The Donkey & Buskins

LAYER-DE-LA-HAYE

N

B1026

Blind Knights

Abberton Reservoir

2 At the end of this road (**Mill Lane**) turn right and very shortly take the footpath on the left between houses. Continue straight down. In front and to the left you will see **Abberton reservoir**. The path turns 90° to the right and out onto the road. Turn right. Immediately tucked behind the thatched cottage is a footpath accessed by a stile. When you reach the bottom go left over another stile and brook and then up a wide grass path. At the shingle path turn right, following this for some distance. Just before the white gate marking the entrance to **Blind Knights Farm**, turn right through a large metal gate.

3 Follow the grassy path over a stile and left down a narrow alley. You are then forced right and into a field. Keep to the right and in the corner take the footpath over another stile into a sheep field. There are wonderful views of the reservoir to the left. Go over two more stiles in quick succession and when you reach the pylon, follow the footpath arrows over more stiles and a wooden bridge. Head towards the church tower. Cross yet more stiles into

the next field and when you cross this one you find yourself at the pretty **church of St John the Baptist** which is usually open if you would like to visit.

Abberton reservoir is home to a variety of wildfowl.

4 Turn left down the main road and a little further down take the footpath on the right. This long path runs close to the edge of the field for some distance and then across the middle of a cornfield to a wide dirt track. This eventually brings you to the road. Turn right and follow this all the way for over a mile. There is little traffic along the lane but watch out for oncoming vehicles, especially on the bends.

5 When you reach the junction, continue round to the right towards **Layer** village. As you enter the village, just after the 30 mph speed sign, take a bridleway on the left through the trees. Bear left into the road at the end, passing cottages and bungalows. The road swings to the right at the end to join the main road. Turn left and continue straight up. The **Donkey & Buskins** is further up on the left-hand side.

Places of interest nearby

Just 2 miles north-east of Layer, on the B1022 (Maldon Road) between Tiptree and Colchester is **Colchester Zoo**. Elephants, giraffes and a white tiger called Sasha are amongst the many animals that can be seen. There are various eating outlets and free parking.
☎ *01206 331292*

7 **Coggeshall**

The White Hart Hotel

Coggeshall **contains over** 100 listed buildings and this is a fascinating walk for anyone with an interest in history. You circumnavigate the town, crossing the River Blackwater and taking winding field paths that pass a medieval Grange Barn, the magnificent parish church, an ancient chapel, the remains of a Cistercian abbey and a mill, as well as many old buildings in the town itself.

THE
PUB

The **White Hart** is a hotel, as well as a pub of character, and parts of the building date from the 15th century. It serves food of a high standard. As well as bar snacks, there is an à la carte, summer salad and a specials menu which changes every week. They flambé the food in the restaurant and the Sunday roasts are carved at the tables. Breakfast is available in the mornings. There is an extensive selection of wines and the beer is Greene King IPA.

Open weekdays from 7.30 am to 11.30 pm and on Saturday and Sunday from 8 am to 11 pm. Food is available in the bar from 12 noon to 2.30 pm and from 6.15 pm to 9.30 pm (7 pm to 9 pm Sunday) and in the restaurant from 12 noon to 2 pm and 7 pm to 9.30 pm (closed Sunday evening).
☎ *01376 561654*

1 From the front of the **White Hart Hotel** on the main road, take the road opposite which is **Market Hill**, signposted to the Council

Distance – 3¾ miles.

OS Explorer 195 Braintree and Saffron Walden. GR 851225.

Good paths and easy walking although the path by the river may be a little heavy going.

Starting point The White Hart Hotel in Coggeshall.

How to get there From the A120 between Braintree and Marks Tey, take the B1024 into Coggeshall town centre. Walkers should ask permission to leave their cars in the hotel car park. There is a free car park in Stoneham Street nearby.

Offices and the Village Hall. After passing a chapel, turn left at the library in **Stoneham Street**. Follow the path that runs alongside a stone wall marked by yellow footpath arrows, and over a little bridge crossing the stream. This brings you to a footpath junction where the route is straight on through a field. After a little wood, take the path that goes left by a horse chestnut tree and then straight on through a field. Go straight over the tarmac track and into a grass field with a red brick wall on the left. You will soon reach the main road.

2 Cross over and turn right, then immediately left, taking the footpath next to the football pitches. Then go into a field of ash trees that soon follows the line of the stream. The path deviates somewhat from the true line of the footpath marked on the OS map and it can be a little difficult in places, being narrow or overgrown. This winding path eventually allows you to cross the

The medieval Grange Barn, passed on the walk.

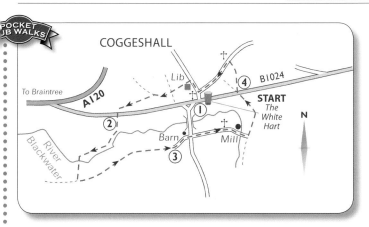

Paycocke's House.

River Blackwater by means of a rickety bridge. Continue to the next bridge, which crosses a dry brook and go uphill to a wide dirt track. Here turn left and follow this for about ¾ mile towards

Coggeshall. This is part of the **Essex Way** (represented by the sign of the poppies). It takes you past Coggeshall's **Grange Barn,** owned by the National Trust.

3 At the road soon after the barn, go straight over and continue past the little abbey gatehouse chapel, built in 1220, and down the private road which is part of the **Essex Way**. The path winds past the privately-owned Cistercian abbey remains and the mill by the stream. At a footpath junction turn left alongside the horse field, with a ditch to your left, still following the **Essex Way National Trail**. At the concrete track by the **Anglian Waterworks**, go straight on over the stile, and on through a metal swing gate to the road.

4 Turn left and a short way down the road, opposite a red brick house, turn into the park on the right. Do not follow the concrete path but instead stay to the right alongside the hedge and then a wire fence, bringing you to a road opposite the magnificent **parish church of St Peter**, worth a visit if you have time. Turn left down the road, passing the shops and many old houses, back to the road junction opposite the **White Hart**.

Places of interest nearby

The **Grange Barn** (NT), which you pass along the way, dates from the 13th century and is associated with the abbey. It has been restored using many of the original timbers.
☎ *01376 562226*

Paycocke's House (NT) in Coggeshall, further along the main road (B1024) towards Braintree, was built by the Paycocke family, rich wool merchants who lived in the village. Inside there is rich panelling and wood carving and a display of lace. Outside is a pretty cottage garden.
☎ *01376 561305*

POCKET PUB WALKS

8 High Roding

The Black Lion

Starting from the heart of the little village of High Roding, this walk takes you to the neighbouring village of Aythorpe Roding. Both villages lie on the old Roman road to Dunmow and have pretty and ancient parish churches which are hidden in country lanes, and both are rivals when it comes to village cricket! Aythorpe Roding has the advantage of a splendid windmill, built in 1779, which still has turning sails.

Distance – 5¼ miles.

OS Explorer 183 Chelmsford and The Rodings. GR 603173.

Fairly flat and easy walking on good paths with a little uneven ground on one path towards the end.

Starting point The free car park in High Roding village.

How to get there High Roding lies on the B184, a Roman road, between Leaden Roding and Great Dunmow. The car park is off the main road shortly after the Black Lion pub, heading north.

THE PUB The **Black Lion** is an impressive looking and wonderful 14th-century coaching inn. It serves a good Sunday lunch and the choices include the usual snacks, a children's menu and a specials board with several options. There are also appetising desserts such as sorbet, cheesecakes and Belgian waffles. The beer is Greene King IPA, plus at least one guest beer such as Speckled Hen. There is a good selection of wines.

Open Monday to Friday 12 noon to 3 pm and 6 pm to 11 pm and all day Saturday and Sunday from 12 noon through until 11 pm. Food is served from 12 noon to 2 pm every day and from 7 pm to 9 pm.
☎ *01371 872847*

1 At the back of the car park, take the footpath across the field keeping a ditch to your right. At the corner of the field go right through the hedge and over the ditch, which is now on the left. As the hedge ends, go left over the ditch again via some wooden planks. A hundred yards or so down the field, look out for a gap

in the hedge to your right with more planks taking you back across the ditch, so that you are now walking the other side of the hedge. A footbridge further down forces you left. The grass path then swings left. Go to the right side of the hedge, still keeping the ditch to the left. This path later joins a wide dirt track. Proceed straight on up, and after some distance you will come to farm buildings (**High Rodingbury Farm**).

2 At the farm, keep to the left alongside the hay barn to a tarmac lane where you turn right past **Bury Cottage**. Continue down the lane, passing a pretty chapel and a metal gate. The path swings

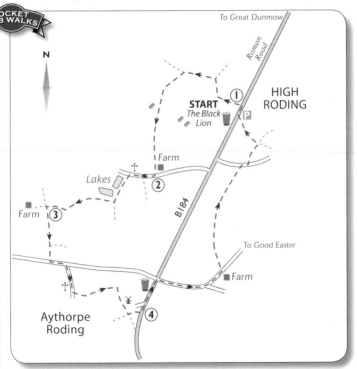

The post mill at Aythorpe Roding.

left past the lakes. After the second lake, at a footpath junction, go right and proceed along the edge of the field with the ditch to your right, to a large oak where the path swings around the edge of the field and eventually joins a bridleway.

3 Turn left, heading towards the church spire. When you reach the lane turn left and at the road junction go right towards **Aythorpe**

Roding. Pass the church and just after a wooden gate to the farm, turn left. There is a deep ditch to the right and soon the windmill comes into view. At a footpath junction by the railway sleepers, turn right towards the windmill. Keep the hedge to your left. Go round the windmill and straight on to the end of the field, then left to the village hall by the road.

4 Turn left and proceed up the main road to the crossroads by the **Axe and Compasses** pub. Here turn right and walk down the lane to the next junction. Go left towards **Good Easter** and when you reach **Bigod's Farm** take the footpath on the left by a little pond. It appears to matter little which side of the ditch you decide on, as on both sides the ground is a little uneven and soft in wet weather. After about two-thirds of a mile, this eventually brings you to a little road leading up to the farm. Turn right, then immediately left down another footpath alongside a tall hedgerow. At the footpath crossroads turn left, following the hedge round and heading towards modern houses by the meadow. When you reach a residential cul-de-sac, turn left at the end, bringing you to the main road. The car park is to the right but turn left for the **Black Lion** and a well-earned pint!

Places of interest nearby

The **windmill in Aythorpe Roding** is a large post mill now leased to Essex County Council. It is open to the public on the last Sunday of every month between April and September from 2 pm to 5 pm. Free admission.
☎ 07887 662177

In Great Dunmow, 2 miles north of High Roding, a visit to the **Maltings** is worthwhile. A 16th-century building houses the town museum, which illustrates the history of Dunmow since Roman times and is open at weekends and at other times during the summer.
☎ 01371 878979

9 **Pleshey**

The White Horse

Pleshey is a small rural village deep in the peaceful heart of the Essex countryside. It is dominated by the earthworks and ramparts of its motte and bailey castle, but has many other old buildings and cottages, some thatched, and a fine 12th-century church almost opposite the White Horse. The surrounding area is ideal for walkers and there is an extensive network of footpaths and bridleways, giving plenty of different

Pleshey Walk 9

Distance – 5½ miles.

OS Explorer 183 Chelmsford and The Rodings. GR 664144.

Mostly very good tracks and paths with some gentle slopes.

Starting point The White Horse in Pleshey.

How to get there *Pleshey is about 5 miles north-west of Chelmsford. From the A130 between Chelmsford and Great Dunmow, turn off at Howe Street and follow the road another 2½ miles west to Pleshey. Walkers may use the pub car park with permission. Street parking in the village is also possible.*

routes to choose from. This circuit takes the walker from the heart of Pleshey along part of the Essex Way, to the neighbouring village of Great Waltham and returns along the ridge, enjoying views across open countryside.

THE PUB The **White Horse** pub dates back to the late 15th century and some of the original timbers and flooring can still be seen inside. It is an excellent freehouse with some unusual features, and is very rambler friendly. There is a gift shop inside which sells souvenirs, cards, candles and the like. Most of the table space is given over to eating as it is as much of a restaurant as it is a pub. There are four menus, no less: bar snacks, à la carte, specials (paying a set price for any two courses), and also a seafood menu. The almond nut roast, casserole of duckling and Mike's Hot and Cold Lobster are amongst the choices. The pub especially caters for those who have an allergy to wheat flour and many dishes are gluten free. Younger's Bitter is served and there is an extensive wine list.

Essex

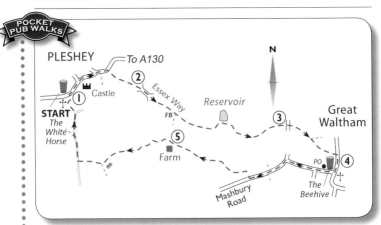

POCKET PUB WALKS

PLESHEY =To A130

N

②

Essex Way

Castle

Reservoir

START
The
White
Horse

FB

Great
Waltham

③

⑤
Farm

PO ④

The
Beehive

Mashbury
Road

Open 11.30 am to 3 pm every day except Sunday, which is 12 noon to 5 pm, and from 6.30 pm to 11 pm Thursday through to Saturday only. Closed in the evenings from Wednesday to Sunday. Food is served 12 noon to 3 pm and from 6.30 pm to 9.30 pm.
☎ *01245 237281*

---

1 Turn left out of the **White Horse** car park and head down the road towards the centre of the village. Continue past the **Leather Bottle** pub and pretty cottages and houses. At the other end of the village, shortly after **Mount House**, take a footpath on the right, with an **Essex Way** sign, which runs along the wire fence of the **Anglian Water Company** property. After leaving the fence the path continues through open fields, following the line of the overgrown brook to your left.

2 At a footpath junction the path crosses a brook, which you then keep to your right. After about ½ mile you will reach a stone bridge where you are diverted left, the path soon swinging to the right through longer grass, and then bending right again by

the reservoir which is concealed behind bushes to your left. After passing the little field of grape vines you are diverted right again, back towards the brook and a pond.

3 When you reach the road, go straight over and continue along the **Essex Way** footpath. After another ½ mile the path brings you over a stile and to the road leading to the village of **Great Waltham**. Turn right down the road. If you need a rest, you are invited to sit in a little garden to your right. Continue to the junction with the **Beehive pub** and the church.

4 Turn right down **Barrack Lane**, passing the post office. Go all the way down the lane to the next junction and here you bear left down **Mashbury Road** (towards **Chignals**). Soon you are out

Holy Trinity parish church, Pleshey.

into open countryside again. Take the public bridleway on the right and follow this wide track for nearly 1 mile, enjoying some good views to your right.

5 When you reach **Fitzjohn's Farm**, at a footpath junction, turn right, then immediately left. Before long you will have a distant view of **Holy Trinity church**. The path winds along the top of the ridge for some distance. When you finally reach the fork junction, go right and continue to the next T-junction where you turn right again, down a concrete path. Follow this all the way heading for **Holy Trinity church** (ignore the turning to the left). At the top of the slope, as the path veers to the right, go left into the cricket ground. Follow round the outside of the field to the gravel path. Turn left and this brings you back to the village street where you will see, to your left, the **White Horse** pub.

Places of interest nearby

Because **Pleshey Castle** is privately owned, viewing is only possible by appointment. It was built by Geoffrey de Mandeville who fought at the Battle of Hastings. The huge motte was one of the biggest in England and is now reached by a 15th-century brick bridge.
☎ 01245 353066

Hylands House and Park are 6 miles to the south of Pleshey, on the south-west outskirts of Chelmsford. The house, owned by Chelmsford District Council, was originally built in 1730 but has undergone many changes since then and is now in the final stages of restoration. It is open on Sunday and Monday. The park of over 500 acres, which is open free all year round, contains woodland, lakes, pleasure gardens, a play area, toilets and free parking, and there are plans for a new visitor centre with café, gift shop and craft studios.
☎ 01245 605500

10 **Stow Maries**

The Prince of Wales

The **tiny village of** Stow Maries consists of a pub, a church
and little else! Its name is derived from the Mareys family
who lived there in ancient times. You pass the pretty little
church on the way through a golf course to the neighbouring
village of Purleigh, which is not much bigger. There you pass All
Saints' church, built mostly in the 14th century, and the nearby
Purleigh Hall which has been tastefully converted but was once
the manor house of the village. Purleigh's elevated location gives
some good views of the surrounding area and the river valley on
the return to Stow Maries.

The **Prince of Wales** pub is approximately 200 years old and
the discovery of an old oven during renovation is evidence
that it may have been a bakery in former times. It is a

freehouse of character, whose owner likes to provide something a little different and is somewhat of a beer expert himself. There is always a selection of draught ales which changes throughout the year but a couple of popular regulars are Caledonian Deuchers and Hop Back Summer Lightning, and draught cider is also available. The bar menu includes the Dengie Geezer (ham and melted cheese on a chapati or baguette), and there is also a specials board. On summer Sundays there is a barbecue, but specializing in fish rather than meat. It is not unusual for fresh barracuda to be on the coals!

Open 12 noon to 11 pm every day except Sunday (closes 10.30 pm). Food is served from 12 noon until about 2.30 pm but there is also a big breakfast served on Sunday at 10 am.
☎ *01621 828971*

Distance – 5¼ miles.

OS Explorer 175 Southend-on-Sea and Basildon, 183 Chelmsford and The Rodings. GR 830993.

Some brief up and down stretches with a little road walking.

Starting point The Prince of Wales in Stow Maries.

How to get there The Prince of Wales is situated on the Stow road, between South Woodham Ferrers and Cold Norton. After leaving South Woodham Ferrers on the B1012 take the turning left signposted to Stow Maries and Cold Norton. The pub is about ½ mile before the village. Walkers have permission to leave vehicles in the pub car park. Otherwise, there is parking further up the road in the village.

POCKET
PUB WALKS

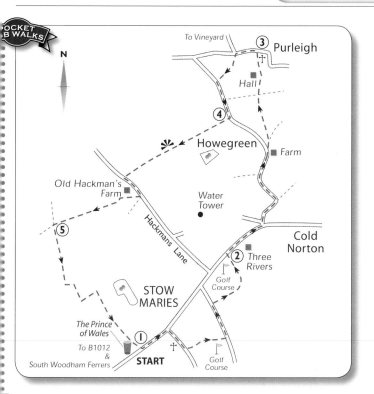

To Vineyard

③ Purleigh

N

Hall

④

Howegreen

Farm

Old Hackman's
Farm

Water
Tower

⑤

Hackmans Lane

Cold
Norton

**② Three
Rivers**

Golf
Course

STOW
MARIES

The Prince
of Wales

①

To B1012
&
South Woodham Ferrers

START

Golf
Course

Turn left out of the **Prince of Wales** car park and walk along the **Stow** road towards the village of **Stow Maries**, going gently uphill. At the top of the hill, take the first turning on the right into **Church Lane**. Pass the pretty **church of St Mary and St Margaret** on your right. A little further down the lane, take the footpath on the left by **Jubilee Cottage**, which takes you alongside the golf course. Cross two fairways (watch out for flying golf balls!) and bear right where you come to an opening onto a tarmac lane. Turn left and walk down the lane. Further up on the right you will see a footpath alongside the 16th hole. Continue straight down and turn left by the little bridge, which takes you past the

1st hole, over a stile and through two sets of open gates to the main road.

2 Turn right past the thatched cottage and the **Three Rivers Country Club**. At the road junction turn left into **Howe Green Road** towards **Purleigh**. There are good views to the left of the countryside

All Saints' church dates from the 14th century.

towards **Woodham Ferrers**. Follow the road as it bends sharply to the left. Watch out for oncoming traffic around the next bend, the road swinging to the right. Just past **Howe Green Farm**, take a footpath on the right – there are actually two footpaths here, marked by posts at openings at the bottom of the little field. Take the left-hand path, through a thicket and over a little footbridge into a large open field. Go straight over, uphill to a stile (which can be seen to the left of the church tower). Go straight over into another little field and over another stile at the end. Follow a concrete track passing **Purleigh Hall**, and go left through the church gate by the postbox. Go round the church and out onto the road on the other side.

3 Turn left onto the road, going downhill to the junction at the bottom. Here turn left, following the footpath sign down a tarmac track. Keep to the left of a wire fence. Ignore a footbridge on the left but go past the children's play area and round the sports field. In the far corner, turn left onto the road. Continue along the road to the top of the incline and just as the road begins to descend, take a footpath on the right, alongside a wooden fence.

4 Follow the yellow footpath arrows straight up. Go through a hedgerow and over a footbridge at the end of the next field, continuing on a gradual uphill gradient all the way, giving good views of the Essex countryside all around. Then go downhill for another third of a mile to the road. Here turn left down **Hackmans Lane**, passing **Old Hackman's Farm**. After about another 150 yards, turn right onto a footpath. There are two paths here again – take the one which veers to the right, close to the line of telegraph wires. This takes you through a gap in the wooden fence, then over another fence. Keep to the left of the hedgerow. At the little footbridge, go straight on into the open field and at the footpath crossroads at the next stile, turn left.

5 The ground close to the fence is rather uneven so for more comfortable walking try to find a route away from the fence which is a little easier. At the next stile follow the yellow footpath arrows left into the next field. The path then veers 90° to the right. It continues to swing left and right until you have a fine view of the **Crouch river valley** ahead. As you now descend, the sight of the **Prince of Wales** pub will motivate you to quicken your step! At the bottom, climb over the wooden stile, then two more stiles to the road and that well-earned beer!

Places of interest nearby

About 5 miles south-east, the other side of Woodham Ferrers is **Battlesbridge Antiques and Craft Centre**.
☎ *01268 575000*

But for something a little different try the **New Hall Vineyards** at Purleigh, close by (see map). There is free wine tasting and a chance to purchase any of the eleven different bottled wines. There is a popular wine festival during the first week in September, or watch how the wine is made in October.
☎ *01621 828343*

11 Mill Green, Ingatestone

The Viper

Mill Green, which lies north of the ancient town of Ingatestone, is more of an area than a village. It is very much horse country, walkers using some of the many bridlepaths that traverse the countryside. The walk goes to Fryerning through lovely farmland and wooded areas. Part of the route is along St Peter's Way, one of the primary Essex walkways. You may choose to do the shorter walk or continue for an extra loop of 1½ miles across fields and through woodland, where you may be lucky enough to spot wild deer.

THE PUB The **Viper** claims to be the only public house of that name in the country. In a very pleasant setting surrounded by trees, it is a quiet and friendly freehouse. It serves several draught ales, including the specially brewed V.I.P.A., which is very tasty! Snacks are available, plus a changing specials menu with several good choices such as steak and ale pie.

Opening hours 12 noon to 3 pm and 6 pm to 11 pm during the week but all day at the weekend from 12 noon onwards. Food is served at lunchtime only from 12 noon to 2 pm except Sunday, when serving hours extend until 3 pm.
☎ *01277 352010*

Distance – 3¼ or 5¾ miles.

OS Explorer 183 Chelmsford and The Rodings. GR 640018.

The route consists of gentle up and down walking with a number of stiles.

Starting point The free parking area opposite the Viper pub at Mill Green.

How to get there *Come off the A12 at Ingatestone. Mill Green is about 1½ miles north of the town on Ingatestone Road. The car park is on common ground by the trees.*

1 From the car park opposite the **Viper**, go left down the tree-lined road. After passing some cottages, turn right down **Maple Tree Lane**. As the lane swings to the right, after the bridleway, go left over a stile (**St Peter's Way**) into a meadow. Bear right, going diagonally across the middle of the field to a stile next to the iron

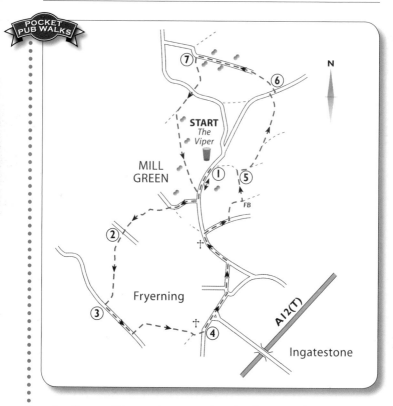

gate, then walking up between the wire fences and over another stile. Keep to the left of the little copse and a water trough and over three more stiles to the road.

2 Take the footpath almost opposite alongside **Barns Farm**, over a stile and into a field. Keep close to the hedge on the right and in the corner of the field go over a little wooden walkway and a stile. Then walk alongside a wire fence to a footbridge and stile over the brook. Follow the footpath arrows up the farm track and through the buildings of **Spring Farm** to the road.

3 Turn left and proceed down the road to the dip where, at the bottom, you turn left along an unmarked footpath by a green gate. Take the path between the ditch and the fence. This soon turns 90° right and over a footbridge, passing a lake on the left. When you reach an open field, go directly across, heading towards the **church of St Mary the Virgin**. At the large

Ingatestone Hall.

oak tree, follow the path past a pond and continue through a swing gate towards the church, whose nave dates from the 11th century, and on through the churchyard. Go past the entrance to the church and out onto the road.

4 Turn left to the road junction by the **Woolpack restaurant**. If you need a rest, there is a seat next to a large oak on the triangular green. Keep left and follow the sign to **Highwood** and **Writtle**. At the next junction continue down **Mill Green Lane** and keep following the signs to **Highwood**. Shortly after the water tower and Gospel Hall, turn right down **Hardings Lane**. Take the footpath on the left (**Mill Green circular walk**) by the little airfield. Go down and over a stile, the path then swinging round to the right. Further down, slightly concealed on the left, is the footpath taking you over the brook via a footbridge and into a horse field. Go over a stile at the end, crossing a track and follow the winding footpath through woodland, guided by numerous **St Peter's Way** footpath posts to another tarmac track. Here, *to finish the shorter walk*, go left, which takes you directly back to your starting place.

5 *To continue the walk*, turn right and then immediately left at the fork, taking the shingle path to **Richard's Cottage**. At the next fork by a metal barrier go left. This soon takes you over a stile and alongside a wire fence. Then go over two more stiles and into an open field. Here you head straight across the field along a wide grass strip, going gently downhill. At the bottom stay to the left alongside a farm fence, which takes you to the road.

6 Turn right and very soon, opposite two houses, go left through a gap in the hedge and across a field to a ditch, where you will spot a little footbridge. This takes you across into an open field where there is no distinct path and the walking is a little rough, but head towards a white painted post by the trees. The path continues through the woods. Follow the footpath arrows over ditches and wooden planks (watch out for wild deer) until you reach the footpath junction close to the cottages.

7 Turn left, following the bridleway. At the bottom, before the brook, the path has been diverted. Go right, following the blue arrows. Cross the ditch into a field, now keeping the ditch to the right until you reach the opening by the road. Cross over and take the bridleway opposite. Cross the field and when you reach the trees, go left at the footpath fork. This takes you first down, then back uphill through the trees. When you finally reach the road, turn left and within about five minutes of walking along the road you will return to the **Viper** pub.

Places of interest nearby

Half a mile south-east of Ingatestone lies **Ingatestone Hall**, a fine, red-brick, Tudor manor house which has been in the hands of the Petre family since its construction. It has gardens, a tea room, free car park and a gift shop. It opens weekend afternoons in the summer.
☎ *01277 353010*

12 **Kelvedon Hatch**

The Dog & Partridge

Kelvedon Hatch **is not to be** confused with the village of Kelvedon on the other side of the county. This short walk goes via the village of Doddinghurst with its ancient parish church which is often open, so visit if you have time. From there the route is through some tranquil Essex countryside back to Kelvedon Hatch.

Distance – 3½ miles.

OS Explorer 175 Southend-on-Sea and Basildon. GR 575985.

The walking is fairly flat and easy with no stiles.

Starting point The Dog & Partridge pub at Kelvedon Hatch.

How to get there *Kelvedon Hatch is on the A128 between Brentwood and Ongar. On the approach to the town driving north from Pilgrims Hatch go right down Blackmore Road. The pub is a little way down on the left. Walkers should ask permission to leave their cars in the car park. There are also parking spaces on the roads around the pub.*

THE PUB

One of the advantages of using the **Dog & Partridge** is that walkers can arrange their ramble for almost any time of day knowing that when they return to the pub it is likely to be open. This is a friendly pub with a good array of food. Look out for the home-made specials such as steak and kidney pudding and lasagne al forno, and some appetising home-made desserts. The beers include Bombardier. There is a nice garden and a duck pond opposite!

Open 11 am to 11 pm from Monday to Saturday and 12 noon to 10.30 pm on Sunday. Food is served from 12 noon to 8 pm (to 6 pm on Sunday).
☎ *01277 375747*

1 From the entrance to the **Dog & Partridge** turn right down the lane, and continue straight down the public bridleway. At

Eagle Lane turn right and then left, though still on Eagle Lane (a cul-de sac), which takes you into the trees, passing a children's playground and playing field. When you reach the road turn right and follow this tree-lined lane for nearly ½ mile. After you pass **Chivers Road** the lane bends sharply to the right and then comes to a T-junction.

Turn left and immediately on your right take the footpath to **Doddinghurst Place**. After you pass a pond and the house, when you come to an open field, bear left, going diagonally across to a metal gate on the other side. After passing through this gate, the path swings left past another large pond and continues between an electric fence (beware) and the higher wire fence. Follow the footpath arrows to a wooden swing gate by the road. Turn left and follow the road past the primary school and, on the other side, the beautiful **parish church of All Saints**. Opposite the church, just after the village hall, go through another swing gate.

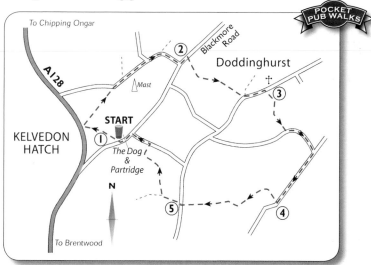

The ancient parish church in Doddinghurst.

3 Bear right, going towards a red litterbin in the far corner of the field, and follow the path through the trees alongside the fence. Then go right across a little wooden bridge and through a wooden gate into a meadow. At the junction of grass paths go straight on, bringing you to a narrow lane where you turn left. Continue to the road junction and turn right. After about ¼ mile, as the lane veers to the right, go through an opening on the right opposite a dirt track. There is no footpath sign here so keep a watchful eye out for this turn.

4 Keep the hedgerow and then the trees to your right. Follow the yellow footpath arrows through a hedge at the end and go left into the next field. At the next corner go through the hedge again over a dry ditch and turn right along the edge of a field, keeping the ditch to your right. Go straight on through the next field and onto a gravel track. Go straight on to the road.

5 Cross straight over and continue along the footpath that goes through a field. At the end, cross over the ditch and turn right heading towards the radio mast and alongside the ditch now to your right. Follow the field boundary round to the left and soon after, just before it bends slightly to the left again, there is a gap through the hedge on the right. It is unmarked and concealed so be careful you don't walk straight past! A short hop across the corner of the next field brings you to a little alley between houses with privet hedges. You then come into a residential road. Take the first turning on the right (**Broad Meadow**) and then left at the end. At the main road turn left towards **Ongar** and the **Dog & Partridge** is a little way down on the right.

Places of interest nearby

Just a mile north of Kelvedon Hatch, with the entrance road off the A128, is the **Secret Nuclear Bunker**. Although secret no longer, it was for many years during the Cold War period, the refuge for prominent members of the government in the event of a nuclear war. Exhibits depict how up to 600 people could have lived underground during such a war. Open daily in the summer, with restricted hours during the winter months.
☎ *01277 364883*

13 Epping Forest

The Owl

Essex still has its ancient forest and is renowned for its ancient trees, in particular, oak, beech and hornbeam. There are over 650 species of plants and the wildfowl on the many lakes and ponds include great crested grebes and herons. This walk follows the main trail, the Green Ride, through the heart of the woodland where royalty from London came to hunt, and later Dick Turpin came to hide after his highwayman escapades. This is a beautiful walk in all seasons, though particularly when the

Epping Forest Walk 13

Distance – 4 miles.

OS Explorer 174 Epping Forest and Lee Valley. GR 399970.

The paths are wide and easy to follow.

Starting point The Owl public house.

How to get there *From the A112 between Chingford and Waltham Abbey, turn off right down Mott Street and at the fork go right down Lippitts Hill. The Owl is about ½ mile along the road on the left. Walkers should ask permission to leave their cars in the Owl car park.*

trees have their autumn colours. The walk passes the Elizabethan Hunting Lodge before returning along a different route to the Owl public house.

THE PUB The **Owl** is situated on a quiet lane in the heart of Epping Forest. If the weather is good, seating outside provides extensive views of the forest and surrounding area. There is a bar menu with plenty to choose from and a good roast on Sunday! If walkers require food at a particular time then they can pre-order by contacting the pub. The beer is McMullen's Best Bitter and there is always a seasonal guest beer also. The pub has its own owl, Charlie, who lives outside in the garden along with some rabbits to keep him company.

Open Monday to Saturday from 11.30 am to 11 pm, Sunday 12 noon to 10.30 pm. Food is served from 12 noon to 3 pm and from 5.30 pm to 9 pm every day.
☎ *0208 502 0663*

1 From the car park of the **Owl** public house, turn right along the road to where it bends to the left (**Elms Park Homes**). Here, turn right down the dirt track and then right again before a metal gate, through a wooden swing gate which takes you between chalets and a horse field. Go through two more swing gates and over a stile to **Church Road**. Here turn right and then immediately left by a metal barrier. Take the wide grass path to the next junction of paths and go right, joining the prominent wide track called the **Green Ride**.

2 Stick to the main path, going straight on in a southerly direction and ignoring all turnings or paths that join the main track.

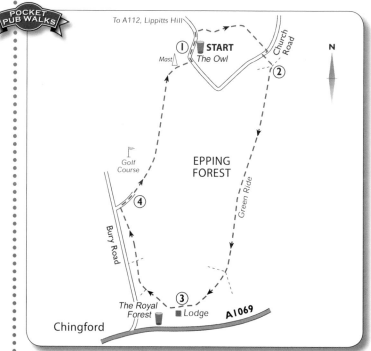

The Elizabethan Hunting Lodge in Epping Forest.

Continue for over 1 mile until eventually you cross a brook and, leaving the trees behind, come to a junction in the open. Take the middle option, along a wide grass path marked by a white post. Follow this gently uphill, taking you towards the white-boarded **Butler's Retreat** restaurant. At the obelisk turn right and continue past the **Elizabethan Hunting Lodge** to the rear of the **Royal Forest** pub car park.

3 From the rear of the car park, bear right, going down the grass path through the field. At the bottom of the slope, cross the ditch and take the path by a white post with a horseshoe. Continue

Essex

to the information board, going straight on along a wide track through the trees. This path is a right of way although it is not clearly marked on the OS map. Go straight over at the footpath crossroads, staying parallel with the road. As the path swings away from the road, go left towards the red postbox. Then turn right down **Hornbeam Lane**.

4 At the end, continue down the private road next to the golf course (public footpath), and over the cattle grid at the bottom to **Ludgate House**. When you reach the car park go through a gate on the left, which has a green 'Warning' sign, and into a field. The path goes gently uphill and eventually divides into three. Take the centre path, which takes you over a stile. Continue on towards the radio mast. The route then swings right, and up steps before reaching the road. Turn left and immediately on the right is the **Owl** public house.

Places of interest nearby

The **Elizabethan Hunting Lodge** was actually built for Henry VIII to use when he was hunting in Epping Forest. This three-storey building now houses a little museum about life in Tudor times and is well worth a visit.
☎ *0208 529 6681*

POCKET PUB WALKS

14 **Herongate**

The Boars Head

THE BOARS HEAD

Herongate's **main claim to fame** is its little cricket ground. The cricket club dates from 1850 and is one of the oldest in the country. From Herongate this walk follows a route to Ingrave through part of Thorndon Park, a 400-acre country park, designated as a Site of Special Scientific Interest. Originally designed by 'Capability' Brown in the 18th century, it includes ancient woodland, deer pastures, hay meadows and wildlife ponds. From Ingrave, you return to

Distance – 5 miles.

OS Explorer 175 Southend-on-Sea and Basildon. GR 632911.

Good paths and easy walking.

Starting point The Boars Head at Herongate.

How to get there Herongate lies on the A128, 3 miles south-east of Brentwood town centre. The Boars Head is on the Billericay road, just off the A128. The pub car park is often busy but it is possible to park around the green and on the side roads close by.

Herongate via Heron Hall, an attractive old farmhouse dating from the late 18th century.

THE PUB **The Boars Head** dates back to Tudor times and was first licensed in the 18th century. It even has its own ghost, said to be that of Dick Turpin. Low ceilings and two open fires add to the atmosphere. It is a popular drinking venue which sells many of the old favourites. The beers are Courage Directors, Wells Bombardier, Greene King IPA and Abbot, and Adnams Broadside. There is a wine list of over 20 wines. The menu has steaks, salads, fish and many other selections which continually vary, but are posted on the specials board in the pub. There is a good children's menu. Outside is a very pleasant seating area overlooking a lake.

Open 11 am to 11 pm. Food is available 11 am to 9.30 pm from Monday to Saturday and 12 noon to 9 pm on Sunday.
☎ *01277 810324.*

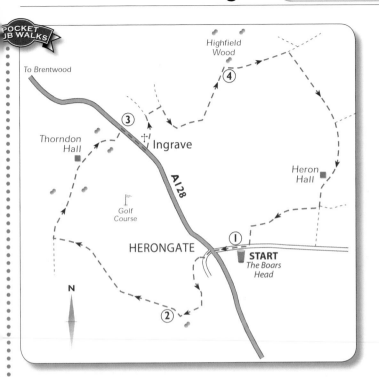

POCKET JB WALKS

To Brentwood

Highfield Wood

④

③

Thorndon Hall

† Ingrave

A128

Heron Hall

Golf Course

HERONGATE

①

START
The Boars Head

N

②

1 Turn left out of the **Boars Head** car park to the main road. Turn right and cross over, walking along the road for a short distance. Just before the bus stop turn left down **Park Lane** and, as the lane bends to the left, bear right to a wooden gate at the entrance to the wood and follow the path through the trees. At the footpath junction by the next wooden gate, turn right, signposted to **Childerditch Street**. Shortly after descending the dip over the brook, turn right over the planks.

2 Proceed between the fence and the golf course. You eventually join a gravel track in the open and later you can choose whether to stay on this path or revert to a parallel path through the woods.

At the next junction, go right along the footpath to **Ingrave**. This takes you through the woods and out to an opening where suddenly in front of you is the magnificent façade of **Thorndon Hall**. The hall was once owned by the Petre family, who now live at Ingatestone Hall. It was damaged by fire in 1878 and left derelict for a century. It is now a private block of luxury flats. Continue to the wooden bridge and soon after you come to the entrance to both the hall and the golf club. Bear left towards the main road at **Ingrave**.

3 Here you turn right and pass the red-brick **church of St Nicholas**. Just the other side, before **School Lane**, take the footpath pointing to **Salmond's Farm** and **Middle Road**. Turn left when you reach the road and then right out of **Salmond's Grove** to

Thorndon Hall, passed on the walk.

a footpath along a tarmac track. Turn right a short way down, along another footpath. At the wooden bridge, go straight on through the hedge and right alongside a large field. There are good views of the countryside to the left. At the next footpath junction turn left and continue towards a wood in the distance. Ignore the first path on the right but take the second one, over a metal bridge.

4 | This is a permissive path not marked on the OS map. It soon follows the line of a ditch. At the next footbridge, turn right along a bridleway. At the footpath crossroads, for a better view of **Heron Hall** go straight over and follow the farm track round to the right. Go through the farm buildings and, after taking a look at this pretty farmhouse, swing left down the narrow lane towards houses in the distance. About halfway down, at a footpath junction, go right alongside two successive fields to **Foucher's Farm**. Here you turn left past the duck pond to the road. Turn right and ahead you will see the sign of the **Boars Head**.

Places of interest nearby

A mile to the west of Thorndon Country Park, at Warley, is the **Brentwood Ski and Snowboard Centre** which is open all year round. There is a go-karting track there too.
☎ *01277 211994*

Close by, also at Warley, is **Brentwood Museum**, which is housed in a picturesque 19th-century building once a sexton's cottage. It offers a fascinating insight into Brentwood life in Victorian times and the early part of the 20th century, with an exciting collection of social and domestic objects dating from around 1840 to 1950.
☎ *01277 224012*

15 **Great Stambridge**

The Cherry Tree

A tranquil stretch of the River Roach is soon reached on this walk from the village of Great Stambridge and if the tide is in it is very pleasant to watch the boats coming and going on the water. The walk begins along Mill Lane, though sadly there is a modern replacement for the tide mill that had stood

Distance – 4½ miles.

OS Explorer 175 Southend-on-Sea and Basildon. GR 891908.

The river path is very good and there is just one stile to negotiate. The last footpath can become a little overgrown in summer.

Starting Point The Cherry Tree at Great Stambridge.

How to get there From Rochford town, north of Southend-on-Sea, follow the signposts on minor roads to Great Stambridge. The Cherry Tree pub is on Stambridge Road about 1 mile outside Rochford. Vehicles can be left in the car park with permission. Alternatively, it is possible to park in Mill Lane (see point 1).

here since Norman times and burned down in 1965. The church, which stands not far from the starting point, is of Saxon origin and is a focal landmark during the walk. The route returns along Bartonhall Creek and along field paths to Great Stambridge.

THE PUB The **Cherry Tree** is a listed 17th-century building, but which has a modern summerhouse extension housing the restaurant. This is a popular eating place, with an extensive menu featuring all the usual favourites, always a specials board, a Sunday roast and a good range of seafood, including trout and sea bass. There is a choice of draught ales, the regular ones being Adnams Broadside and Directors. There are over 24 wines on the menu. The pub is prepared to be a little flexible on its opening times for ramblers, but if you intend to eat there, then it is recommended you reserve a table, as the restaurant is often busy.

Open 12 noon to 3 pm every day except a little later on a Sunday, and from 7 pm to 11 pm. Food can be ordered from 12 noon to 2 pm and from 7 pm to 9 pm.
☎ *01702 544426*

1 Turn right out of the **Cherry Tree** car park and walk down the road towards **Rochford**. Take the first turning on the left down **Mill Lane** (signposted to **Stambridge Mills**). A little way down, where there is a large gap in the hedge, take the footpath on the left, the **Roach Valley Way**, which will bring you to a footbridge and gate over the lakes and on past the cricket ground. Cross over a tarmac track and continue through the gate down to the river.

2 At the river the path swings round to the left and meanders alongside the **River Roach**. Enjoy the tranquillity and, if the tide is in, the boats that go up and down the river. To the left can be seen **Great Stambridge parish church**. Eventually, after about 1 mile, the path swings round to the left once again, away from

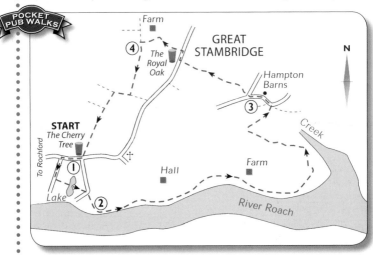

A peaceful scene in Great Stambridge.

the river. Follow the path back along by **Bartonhall Creek**, then it turns sharp right towards **Hampton Barns**. Come off the raised path when you reach a lane and go left following the footpath sign.

3 Go past the farm buildings and, just as the path swings left (before a cattle grid), go right down an unmarked path that passes a small open barn and a line of fir trees on the right. A large pink barn stands on the left. This takes you into an open field. Follow the line of telegraph wires and on to the village of **Great Stambridge**. When you reach the road, turn right and

then left down **Stewards Elm Farm Lane** by the **Royal Oak** pub. Go left just before the iron farm gates and over a footbridge onto a wide grass path. At the end, next to the sports field, go over a stile and turn left.

4. When you reach a field go straight ahead, along a narrow path that cuts right through it. At the end continue straight ahead to a junction of footpaths and turn right along a wide grass path between the crops. After a few hundred yards follow a footpath arrow, turning left down another narrow path. Ignore a turning on the right but continue straight on, keeping the hedgerow to your right. This path, which is sometimes a little overgrown in places, brings you back to the road right next to the **Cherry Tree**.

Places of interest nearby

Three miles south of the Cherry Tree pub, the other side of Rochford at Prittlewell, is **Priory Park** and, within this, the old 12th-century **Cluniac priory** from which the park gets its name. Its museum houses a communications display of early radios, televisions and suchlike. There is also a wildlife exhibition, but the priory itself is the main attraction, part of the building, including the Great Refectory, having survived the dissolution of the monasteries in the 16th century. Within the park lies a recently discovered Saxon burial, thought to be the 7th-century King of Essex, Saebert. Opening hours vary.

☎ 01702 342878 website: www.southendmuseums.co.uk